Witness to History

Pearl Harbor

Gary E. Barr

Heinemann Library
Chicago, Illinois

Customer Service 888-454-2279
Visit our website at www.heinemannlibrary.com

Designed by Heinemann Library
Page layout by Ginkgo Creative, Inc.
Photo research by Alan Gottlieb
Printed and bound in China by South China Printing
Company Limited

08 07 06 05 04
10 9 8 7 6 5 4 3 2 1

**Library of Congress
Cataloging-in-Publication Data**
Barr, Gary, 1951-
    Pearl Harbor / Gary Barr.
        p. cm. -- (Witness to history)
Summary: Uses primary source materials to study what
led to the Japanese attack on Pearl Harbor and the
repercussions of this event.
Includes bibliographical references and index.
    ISBN 1-4034-4569-9 -- ISBN 1-4034-4577-X (PB)
    1. Pearl Harbor (Hawaii), Attack on, 1941--Juvenile
literature. 2. World War, 1939-1945--Causes--Juvenile
literature. 3. United States--Foreign relations--Japan--
Juvenile literature. 4. Japan--Foreign relations--United
States--Juvenile literature. [1. Pearl Harbor (Hawaii),
Attack on, 1941--Sources. 2. World War,
1939-1945--Causes--Sources. 3. United States--Foreign
relations--Japan--Sources. 4. Japan--Foreign relations--
United States--Sources.] I. Title. II. Witness to history
(Heinemann Library
(Firm))
    D767.92.B342 2004
    940.54'26693--dc22

2003018147

Acknowledgments
The author and publisher would like to thank the
following for permission to reproduce photographs:

pp. 4, 33, 36, 43, 44, 46, 51 National Archives and
Records Administration; pp. 5, 16, 19, 24, 30 Naval
Historical Center; pp. 6, 7, 12, 18, 21, 25, 38, 42
Bettmann/Corbis; p. 11 National Portrait Gallery,
Smithsonian Institution/Art Resource; p. 13 Hugo
Jaeger/Time Life Pictures/Getty Images; pp. 20, 31, 34, 40
Hulton Archive/Getty Images; p. 22 Harris & Ewing/
Franklin D. Roosevelt Library; p. 23 Thomas D. McAvoy/
Time Life Pictures/Getty Images; p. 27 Maps.com/Corbis;
p. 29 Library of Congress; pp. 35, 49 Corbis; pp. 45, 50
Carl Mydans/Time Life Pictures/Getty Images

Cover photograph of Pearl Harbor taken by surprise
during the Japanese aerial attack, reproduced with
permission of National Archives and Records
Administration.

The publisher would like to thank Guy LoFaro for his
help in the preparation of this book.

Disclaimer
All the Internet addresses (URLs) given in this book
were valid at the time of going to press. Due to the
dynamic nature of the Internet, however, some
addresses may have changed, or sites may have ceased
to exist since publication. While the author and
publisher regret any inconvenience this may cause
readers, no responsibility for any such changes can
be accepted by either the author or the publisher.

Some words are shown in bold,
like this. You can find out what
they mean by looking in the glossary.

Contents

Introduction

President Franklin D. Roosevelt called the day "a date which will live in **infamy**." On December 7, 1941, Japanese planes bombed Pearl Harbor, the American naval base in Oahu, Hawaii. The following day, he declared war on Japan and brought the United States into the global conflict known as World War II (1939–1945).

How did the Japanese destroy much of the United States Navy in just minutes? Why did they attack? Did the United States make mistakes that provoked this tragedy? What can be learned from Pearl Harbor?

Many Japanese people felt their attack was a huge victory against a nation that had caused them great difficulties. Americans felt that Japan had lied and been ruthless in the Pearl Harbor attack, which killed more than 2,000 people. Was this a brilliantly planned and executed attack by the Japanese? Or did a series of errors made by the United States lead to this disaster? The answer to both questions is yes.

President Franklin D. Roosevelt signs the declaration of war against Japan on December 8, 1941.

The assault on Pearl Harbor caused resentment that remains today. It is difficult for numerous Americans to forgive Japan because so many lives were lost. Meanwhile, many Japanese feel they were compelled to go on the offensive and bomb Pearl Harbor in order to secure the gains they had already made in their wars of conquest in Asia.

When Japanese military leaders began to gain control of their government in the 1930s, Japan's relationship with the United States quickly **deteriorated.** Soon, the Japanese leaders felt that the only solution to their problems was to declare war. After invading northern China, Japan became determined to conquer other lands in Southeast Asia. To do this, they would need to eliminate the main defense for those lands—the United States Navy.

This is an aerial view of Pearl Harbor and Hickam Field on October 13, 1941, before the Japanese attack.

Learning About the Past

By studying history, we learn about events of the past. For example, if we need to learn about the fall of the **Roman Empire** or the arrival of Europeans in the United States, we can find many books and articles about the subjects. Books and articles tell us when and how these events took place, as well as who were the leading characters. These sources often explain not only why things happened—by giving the background to the events—but also how the events changed the course of history.

Although these works are helpful and informative, they are often written many years—sometimes many centuries—after the actual events took place. Like any story that is told secondhand, some changes can creep into the accounts. A historian's mindset can affect how the story is told, because the facts are presented as he or she wanted them to occur. A historian might also leave out some of the facts that do not fit into his or her worldview. Such a personal opinion is called **bias,** and it makes some historical accounts unreliable. However, a historian may have no personal opinion on the matter,

Headlines like this were in newspapers around the country following the attack.

Members of the U.S. Navy gather to read details about the attack on Pearl Harbor. The United States tried to stay out of World War II, but this attack changed people's minds.

but might still rely on other accounts that were written long after the events took place. Such accounts are called secondary sources, because a historian arrives at them secondhand. Here again one must take care in deciding on the truth. Historians who base their writing on earlier retellings might be repeating the bias or even the mistakes of the previous accounts. It is easy to see how through this process, a simple statement could change with each retelling.

Primary sources are firsthand accounts of events. Historians dealing with events from long ago must rely on primary sources. Some examples of primary sources are codes of law, religious registers, letters, journals, and diaries. Many people kept a record of events from their viewpoint. These firsthand accounts give us an up-close, personal view of a certain time period.

Geography of the Pacific

Pearl Harbor is on Oahu, Hawaii's most populated island. The harbor is located at a place where the Pearl River and other streams meet the Pacific Ocean. Ford Island is in the middle of Pearl Harbor. Several important United States naval facilities were located there in 1941. Hawaii's largest city, Honolulu, is ten miles (sixteen kilometers) southeast of Pearl Harbor.

The Hawaiian Islands, near the center of the Pacific Ocean, had gained importance as a United States military base and as a center of international trade. Although Honolulu was the largest city in Oahu, Pearl Harbor was a better place for ships to **dock.** This is because the **bay** of Pearl Harbor has deep, calm water. Ships can load and unload at Pearl Harbor much more easily because waves do not strike ships as they would along Honolulu's shoreline.

Thousands of islands dot the Southwest Pacific region. Countries such as Indonesia, the Philippines, and Australia are rich in minerals and other important **raw materials,** which are shipped to other countries to sell. Like Hawaii, these islands are mountainous and have **tropical climates.**

At the time of the attacks on Pearl Harbor, goods and people were transported across the Pacific Ocean by ships. In the 1940s airplanes were not able to carry enough fuel to cover long distances. Therefore, in a wartime situation, the key to controlling the Pacific region would be a strong naval force. Even if an army controlled an island, large ships could attack it with their huge guns. With the support of aircraft carriers, fighter planes and bombers could be launched nearer to such targets. World War II in the Pacific was predominately a naval war because of the military's dependence on ships.

An American's impression of Hawaii

This excerpt from *Fortune* magazine in 1940 reflects the average American's view of Hawaii before the Pearl Harbor attacks. Hawaii was not yet a state—it did not become one until 1959—but was a U.S. territory at the time.

Decades of advertising and movie iteration [promotions] have convinced practically every stranger outside the islands that Hawaii is still a semi-civilized Eden [paradise]. . . . [But] Hawaii—or the island of Oahu—is first of all a fort . . . [that] gives us a long jump on the Japanese when and if the great Pacific War of the future breaks out.

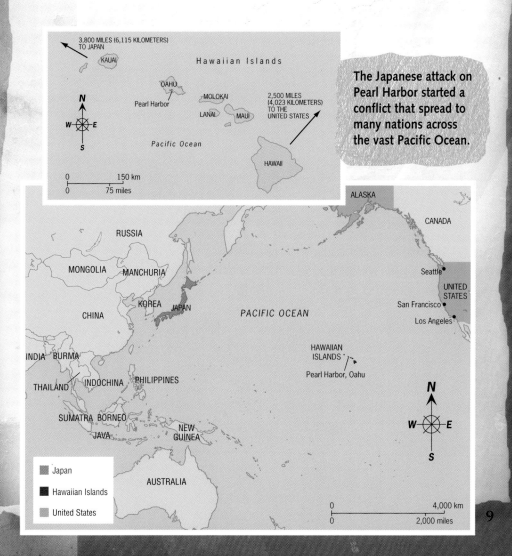

The Japanese attack on Pearl Harbor started a conflict that spread to many nations across the vast Pacific Ocean.

Japan: 1853-1930

For hundreds of years, Japan was a world of its own. Almost no foreigners were allowed to live there. Most Japanese believed outsiders would disrupt their lifestyle. To many Japanese, foreigners were **barbarians.**

Sudden and drastic changes occurred in Japan during the 1800s. In 1853, Commodore Matthew Perry of the United States Navy sailed into the harbor of Tokyo, Japan. His orders were to force the Japanese to trade with the United States. The United States wanted to sell its goods to the Japanese at a **profit.** Because Perry's **fleet** possessed better weapons, Japan was eventually forced to **comply.**

By the 1880s, Japanese trade expanded very quickly. The Japanese liked the modern products they acquired from other countries. New factories were built in Japan to produce these products. However, there was one major problem—Japan lacked many **natural resources.** This meant the country did not have the basic materials necessary to make steel, fuels, and other products needed to make factory goods. Trading for these materials was expensive. Restrictive trade **policies** enforced by other nations during the **Great Depression** (1929–1939) harmed Japan's **economy.** During the Depression, many countries put high taxes on goods they **imported.** This made it very hard for Japan's companies to sell their products to other nations.

By the early 1900s, military **dictators** began to gain control of Japan. Their goal was to build Japan into a world power. Japan's factories began producing large amounts of modern weapons, and the armed forces were expanded. At the same time, military dictators promised the Japanese people a better life. They developed plans to conquer other nations. Leaders demanded trade agreements with nations that would give advantages to Japan. When Japan invaded several areas in Asia, the United States grew worried. The U.S. worked to further weaken the Japanese economy by cutting off supplies of oil, scrap metal (useful in making many products), and other materials.

An ambassador's account

Edwin Reischauer was the United States **ambassador** to Japan in the early 1900s. Reischauer, whose parents had taught in Japan for many years, became an expert on Japanese-American relations.

Matthew Perry gave Japan until Spring of 1854 to accept demands for opening their harbors to American trade. In 1854 the Treaty of Kanagawa was signed. The vast majority of the [Japanese] people, long accustomed to isolation from the rest of the world, were bitterly opposed to allowing foreigners into their land. Once the door had been pushed open a crack, there was no closing it. . . . The European powers soon made similar treaties with Japan, and the door [for trade] was wide open.

During the second half of the nineteenth century, the European powers were engaged in a mad scramble to build up colonial empires by carving out new domains in Africa, Asia, and Oceania [the Pacific region]. . . . They [Japanese leaders] saw that poor and small Japan needed more natural resources to become a first-class world power, and they believed that control of adjacent [nearby] territories would yield many of these resources and strengthen the defenses of Japan. The political and military weakness of China and Korea made these lands ripe [ready] for foreign aggression.

This painting depicts the landing of Commodore Perry to meet Imperial Commisioners at Yoku-hama, Japan, March 8, 1854.

Why Fascism?

Fascism gained popularity in many parts of the world between 1922 and 1945. In a fascist society, a **dictator** controls a nation. A nation is more important than an individual, and all opposition to the leader is harshly suppressed. Fascist leaders often felt that the rest of the world was mistreating their countries. In response, they built up large militaries to fight against this mistreatment.

In 1940 the Japanese signed an agreement with the fascist leaders of two other countries, Benito Mussolini of Italy and Adolf Hitler of Germany. These three nations became known as the **Axis** powers. In 1941, Hideki Tojo, one of Japan's most fanatic leaders, became **prime minister** and took control of the country.

One of the most important reasons why people supported fascist leaders is because the general **standard of living** improved under their leadership. In the early 1900s, Japan's businesses had performed poorly and there was a lack of jobs. Tojo and his followers were able to improve these conditions.

Unfortunately, the result of fascism at that time was World War II (1939–1945). Millions of people would lose their lives in the huge worldwide conflict due to the **expansionist** activities of fascist leaders.

The Japanese military controlled Japan's government by the 1940s. Here Emperor Hirohito (standing on box) and Tojo (bowing) mark the 2,600th anniversary of the founding of the Japanese Empire on October 21, 1940.

Hitler's view of Germans

Adolf Hitler's followers thought that Germans were superior to all others. Hitler required students in Germany to learn that Germans had performed better than all other people throughout history. The following excerpt is from a German science textbook of the 1940s:

The Nordic [German] possesses a feeling for internal and external cleanliness, while the non-Nordic [non-German] always lives in dirt when he is among his own people. . . . All the better developed characteristics are typical of the Nordic body and the Nordic soul. . . . Non-Nordics are more or less equal to the animals or they form a . . . link to them. The Non-Nordic . . . ranks next to the man-apes. He is therefore . . . a . . . sub-man. . . . [The] Nordic man is . . . the creator of all culture and civilization.

Hitler's view of society

While in jail (1923–1924), Hitler wrote a book called *Mein Kampf* (*My Struggle*). In this book, he explained his views on society. The "hammer" that he talks about here refers to powerful leaders; the "anvil" refers to those who must follow because they are weaker.

The whole of nature is a continuous struggle between strength and weakness, an eternal victory of the strong over the weak . . . One is either the hammer or the anvil. We confess that it is our purpose to prepare the German people for the role of the hammer . . . We confess further that we will dash anyone to pieces who should dare to hinder us in this undertaking . . .

Fascists like Hitler often spread their ideas by using violence.

Expansionist Japan: 1930-1941

In 1930 a lawmaking body called the **Diet** controlled Japan. Like the United States Congress, it consisted of two groups, or houses, of lawmakers. The poor **economy** at the time was making life difficult for Japanese citizens—the Diet was unable to provide solutions to the nation's business problems. The Diet soon declined in importance, and military leaders began to gain power.

The military leaders asked the Japanese people to unite behind them so they could expand the country. The leaders promised that businesses would prosper if Japan made better trade agreements and if it took over regions rich in resources. These lands would provide **raw materials** and boost factory production. They would also take in settlers from the overcrowded Japanese cities.

Gradually, the military leaders won the support of the Japanese people. The armed forces were strengthened and modernized. In 1931, the Japanese army invaded a part of China called Manchuria without permission from either the Japanese **prime minister** or the emperor. In 1932 the **League of Nations** called for Japan to leave Manchuria. The Japanese government responded by cutting all ties with that organization in 1933. In 1937, Japanese forces again clashed with China, this time near Peking (modern Beijing). In 1940, Japan signed the Tripartite **Pact** with Italy and Germany, stating that each country would assist the others in the face of foreign aggression. In July of 1941, Japan invaded part of **Indochina,** which included the present-day countries of Cambodia, Laos, and Vietnam.

The United States protested this latest move by cutting off its metal and fuel **exports** to Japan. This was a serious blow to Japan's expansion, because 80 percent of the metal and fuel used by Japan came from the United States. Japanese Prime Minister Konoe tried to **negotiate** a **treaty** with the United States, but they could not agree on terms. Konoe **resigned,** and General Hideki Tojo, the Japanese war minister, became Japan's prime minister as well. Japan then began preparing for a surprise attack against the United States.

A journalist's warning
Early in 1941, Japanese journalist Soho Tokutomi gave a warning to the world.

There is no denying that the seas are high in the Pacific . . . The time has come for the Japanese to make up their minds to reject any who stand in the way of their country . . .

A prediction of war
A prediction of war occurred as early as January 27, 1941. A warning reached **Ambassador** Joseph Grew in Washington, D.C. Experts in Washington read Grew's message, but concluded that an attack would not happen anytime soon.

My Peruvian colleague told a member of my staff that he had heard from many sources, including a Japanese source, that the Japanese military forces planned, in the event of trouble with the United States, to attempt a surprise mass attack on Pearl Harbor using all their military facilities. He added that although the project seemed fantastic, the fact that he had heard from many sources prompted him to pass on the information.

An account of Japanese war preparations
On May 27, 1941, Captain Hideo Hiraide, a Japanese spokesperson, spoke about war preparations on the Tokyo radio station JOAK.

The naval air force has now some 4,000 planes which have constantly been drilling themselves for special war tactics. . . . Thus with a firm conviction and confidence, the Navy is now biding its time with full preparedness . . . to crush in a moment anyone who dares to challenge Japan . . .

Japan's strong military quickly overwhelmed nearby nations.

Japanese Military Strategy

After its military successes in China, Japan decided to expand in another direction—south. The Philippines, Burma, **Indochina,** Indonesia, and other nations south of Japan possessed huge amounts of **natural resources** that Japan wanted. Singapore and Hong Kong had useful harbors that the Japanese military could use.

Admiral Isoroku Yamamoto came up with the idea to attack Pearl Harbor almost a year before the actual attack took place. Early in 1941, Yamamoto was sure that war would eventually erupt between Japan and the United States. He stated, "If we are to have war with America, we will have no hope of winning unless the U.S. **fleet** in Hawaiian waters can be destroyed." Commander Minoru Genda began to draw up attack plans. Spies were used to determine the best time for an attack on Pearl Harbor.

The United States Navy kept its largest number of vessels in Pearl Harbor, on the Hawaiian island of Oahu. At times, more than half of the U.S. Navy was **docked** in the harbor. It made an inviting target. A successful attack could destroy much of the U.S. Navy's fighting capabilities. Japan thought that it would take a long time for the United States to rebuild its navy. During that time, Japan could conquer areas in Southeast Asia and become too strong for anyone to stop them.

This picture shows Admiral Isoroku Yamamoto at work. His ideas led to the deadly Japanese attack on Pearl Harbor.

Japan decided to attack using bombers and fighter planes launched from aircraft carriers. An additional attack would come from **midget submarines.** Hundreds of aircraft would follow different routes at different times to destroy the main ships and airplanes located in and near Pearl Harbor. No ground forces would be involved. The idea was not to invade, but to destroy.

Commander Genda's strategy

Japanese Commander Minoru Genda was asked to identify the attack plan's main features and to make some suggestions. In late February he presented the following **objectives:**

1. The attack must catch the enemy completely by surprise.

2. The main objective of the attack should be U.S. [aircraft] carriers.

3. Another priority target should be U.S. land-based planes on Oahu.

4. Every available [Japanese] carrier should participate in the operation.

5. The attack should utilize all types of bombing—torpedo, dive, and high-level [high **altitude**].

6. Fighter planes should play an active part in the attack.

7. The attack should be made in daylight, preferably in the early morning.

8. Refueling at sea would be necessary.

9. All planning must be done in strict secrecy.

Admiral Yamamoto's orders

The Task Force will launch a surprise attack at the outset of the war upon the U.S. Pacific Fleet supposed to be in Hawaiian waters, and destroy it.

The Task Force will reach the designated stand-by point for the operation in advance.

The date of starting the operation is tentatively set forth as December 8 [December 7 in Hawaii].

U.S. Military Leaders

At the time of Japan's attack on Pearl Harbor, Franklin Delano Roosevelt was president of the United States. As president, he was also **commander in chief** of the U.S. Army and Navy. All U.S. military commanders looked to Roosevelt for direction when the attack came.

Admiral Husband Kimmel commanded the U.S. Pacific **Fleet** stationed in Hawaii. Warned of a possible war with Japan, Kimmel dispatched naval patrols far to the west of Pearl Harbor, in the direction of Japan. These patrols did not detect the Japanese fleet that had circled to the north before launching its attack.

General Walter Short commanded the army forces near Oahu. Short misunderstood messages he received that warned of a Japanese attack. Short assumed that the messages were warning him to protect against **sabotage.** He therefore took appropriate precautions: planes were parked closely together so guards had smaller areas to protect. However, in this formation, bombers attacking from the air could destroy several planes with one properly-dropped bomb.

Kimmel and Short complained that they did not have enough men and equipment to properly defend the area. This was true. Many men and weapons had been transferred from Hawaii to other sites. Most United States leaders did not expect an attack on Pearl Harbor. Also, experts who had discovered Japanese attack plans did a poor job communicating their findings to these two leaders.

Short was Military Governor of Hawaii at the time of the attack on Pearl Harbor.

Interview with Admiral Husband Kimmel

On the morning of December 6, 1941—one day before the attack on Pearl Harbor—Admiral Husband Kimmel gave an interview to Joseph C. Harsch of the newspaper *The Christian Science Monitor.*

Harsch: I know nothing about the situation out here in the Pacific theater [region]. I'll ask the obvious question. Is there going to be a war out here?

Kimmel: No.

Harsch: Would you please explain why you seem so confident that there won't be a war?

Kimmel: Moscow is not going to fall this winter. That means that the Russians will still be in the war in the spring. That means that the Japanese cannot attack us in the Pacific without running the risk of a two-front war. The Japanese are too smart to run that risk.

Admiral Kimmel's excellent performance in the navy resulted in quick promotions.

Interview with General Eisenhower

General Dwight Eisenhower, who later became supreme commander of all **Allied** forces fighting World War II in Europe, was interviewed after the Japanese attack on Pearl Harbor.

I . . . had no idea that battle would be precipitated by the Japanese. If we got into war—and with each passing week I became more and more sure we could not stay out—I felt sure the **Nazis** [Germans] would provoke it.

Japanese Military Leaders

Powerful emperors had ruled Japan for thousands of years. By the 1900s, however, emperors had lost much of their actual power and were looked upon as advisors and symbols of the past. The **prime minister** became the most important Japanese government leader. The prime minister, who was a member of the **Diet,** had a role comparable to that of a United States president.

Emperor Hirohito was 40 years old when Pearl Harbor was attacked. He was very popular with the people of Japan. In their eyes he was more than an emperor, he was a god. Because of this role—although the prime minister and cabinet had to report to him—he was not able to give military leaders direct instructions like the president can to the American cabinet. He had to talk through others.

Prime Minister Hideki Tojo was the man with the most power in Japan during World War II. As a military man, Tojo wanted to make Japan one of the strongest powers on Earth.

Admiral Isoroku Yamamoto was the supreme commander of the Japanese navy. After he joined the Japanese military, he rose through the ranks and became Japan's most respected commander. He built his nation's naval and air force and, though opposed to war with the U.S., felt that if it were to come, Japan must strike first.

Admiral Chuichi Nagumo commanded the Japanese strike force on Pearl Harbor. When others wanted to continue fighting, he halted the attack. This resulted in a failure to find and destroy U.S. aircraft carriers.

Hideki Tojo was not afraid of using violence to achieve his goals. He hated nations that tried to restrict Japan's power.

Admiral Yamamoto's view

Admiral Yamamoto spoke to his aides during the build-up to war:

Gentlemen, you know I'm against war with the United States. But I am an officer of the Imperial Navy, and a subject of His Majesty the Emperor. Recent international events, and developments here at home, make such a war seem almost inevitable [unavoidable], and it is my duty as **commander in chief** *to be ready.*

Emperor Hirohito's view

Emperor Hirohito advised his leaders not to **conquer** other regions. During a September 1941 cabinet meeting, the leaders decided to go to war without Hirohito's approval. Hirohito quoted from a poem written by his grandfather, who questioned the value of conflict when peace was so valuable.

Though I consider the surrounding seas as my brothers
Why is it that the waves should rise so high?

Emperor Hirohito had a life-long interest in biology. Here he sits in his lab in the Akasaka Imperial Palace on January 7, 1926.

The Countdown to War Begins: November 25, 1941

Washington, D.C.:
President Roosevelt and members of his cabinet meet with military leaders. Secretary of State Cordell Hull says that the Japanese appear ready to fight the United States. Leaders of the army and navy both reply that they are not ready. A decision is made to act as though the United States will cooperate with Japanese leaders. Meanwhile, they prepare for war. It is generally agreed that the armed forces will need at least three months to prepare.

Pearl Harbor, Oahu, Hawaii:
Commanders Kimmel and Short are warned that a Japanese attack on Southeast Asia or the Philippines may be likely to happen soon. They had already ordered extensive training of troops in case of an attack on Pearl Harbor, but decided that they did not need to take further precautions at that time.

Northern Japan:
Japanese Admiral Chuichi Nagumo leads his huge **fleet** out of Tankan Bay in the Kurile Islands. Among the 20 ships are 6 aircraft carriers with a total of 414 combat planes on board. They had been training for an attack on Pearl Harbor for months, but only the admiral and a few others knew the details of their mission.

President Roosevelt and his cabinet meet in late 1941 to discuss Japan and World War II.

Secretary of State Hull's view
In January 1941, U.S. Secretary of State Cordell Hull shared
his thoughts about Japan with Lord Halifax, the British
ambassador to the United States.

*There is a real possibility of danger that cannot be
overlooked by any of the peaceful countries. This is that
the military group in control in Japan, by a sudden,
unannounced movement, could any day send an expedition
to the Netherlands, East Indies, and Singapore. Or they
could, inch by inch and step by step, get down to advanced
positions in and around Thailand and the harbor of Saigon,*
Indo-China. *This would leave the peacefully disposed
elements in Japan, including the Japanese Ambassador to
the United States,
to express their
amazement and
to say that
such actions
were without
their knowledge
or consent.*

A Secretary of State is
responsible for foreign
relations **policy** with the
U.S. Here is Secretary of
State Cordell Hull.

Japanese Movements: December 1-2, 1941

December 1, 1941

Japan:

Adolf Hitler, **dictator** of **Nazi** Germany, tells the Japanese that he will support them if they go to war with the United States.

Washington, D.C.:

Japanese **diplomats** say they wish to continue **negotiations** with the United States in order to avoid war. Meanwhile, a secret Japanese message is intercepted by the United States and translated. The message reads "Climb Mount Niitaka!" No one in Washington knows what it means.

North Pacific Ocean:

Admiral Nagumo received the message "Climb Mount Niitaka!" The coded message means "Proceed with attack." Crew members onboard the Japanese **fleet** are given the message. Haruo Yoshino, a Japanese **torpedo** bomber pilot, said "Our fighting spirit was high. There was no question in my mind that we would be successful." The ships turn southeast toward Pearl Harbor.

Admiral Chuichi Nagumo was a highly decorated officer in Japan's navy.

December 2, 1941

Pearl Harbor:

U.S. Admiral Kimmel is told that a huge Japanese attack will be made, but is not told the exact location of the attack. He is also told that a large portion of the Japanese fleet cannot be located. Everyone suspects that a target in Southeast Asia will be attacked.

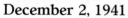

A view of the Japanese Foreign Ministry

Prior to the attacks, the Japanese Foreign Ministry sent a message to **Ambassador** Nomura in Washington, D.C.:

*Commercial and **economic** relations between Japan and third countries, led by England and the United States, are gradually becoming so horribly strained that we cannot endure it much longer. Consequently, our empire, to save its very life, must take measures to secure the **raw materials** of the South Seas. Our Empire must immediately take steps to break asunder [apart] this ever-strengthening chain of encirclement which is being woven under the guidance ... of England and the United States, acting like a cunning dragon seemingly asleep. This is why we decided to obtain military bases in French **Indo-China** and to have our troops occupy that territory ...*

Cordell Hull said Japanese ministers Kichisaburo Nomura and Saburo Kurusu lied, promising peace.

Final Preparations: December 3-6, 1941

December 3, 1941
Pacific Ocean, with the Japanese Fleet:
A message is received from Japanese spies at Pearl Harbor. It details the most current locations of U.S. ships **moored** along the area known as Battleship Row.

Nagumo plans for nine planes to stay with each Japanese aircraft carrier for protection. In the first wave of attack, 189 planes will be launched. **Torpedo** bombers and high **altitude** bombers will target the U.S. battleships. Dive-bombers will attack the airfields. In the second wave of attack, 171 dive-bombers and high-level bombers will finish the destruction. The planes will take off at 6:15 A.M. on December 7, 1941.

December 4, 1941
Pearl Harbor:
Admiral Kimmel has sent planes from aircraft carriers already out in the Pacific Ocean to search for any sign of Japanese ships. These planes fly scouting missions to the west of Hawaii, between Hawaii and Japan. With a limited number of planes, no scouting is done to the north or east of the islands.

December 6, 1941
Washington, D.C.:
Reports of increased Japanese military movements near the Philippines and south of China continue. President Roosevelt decides to personally warn Emperor Hirohito. He says that war will result from any Japanese attack, but adds that peace will result if the Japanese withdraw their forces from Southeast Asia.

Pacific Ocean, with the Japanese Fleet:
Final preparations for the attack are made. By the following morning at 6:00 A.M., the Japanese **fleet** will be only 230 miles (370 kilometers) north of Pearl Harbor.

Pearl Harbor:
U.S. Naval Command continues to be concerned that it is still unable to locate several Japanese ships. Plans are reviewed in case an attack in Southeast Asia occurs. A Japanese message is intercepted that mentions the number of ships in Pearl Harbor along with different types of flowers—some sort of code. The officer discovering the message decides he will tell the Admiral tomorrow.

An ironworker's account

Ed Sheehan, a Pearl Harbor ironworker, was working the night of December 6.

Off Ford Island we could see twinklings from the *Avocet*, *Neosho*, and *California*, and beyond, the beady lights of other battleships. The destroyer *Shaw* and tug *Sotoyomo* presented only a small scattering of lights in the floating **dry-dock**. The chief said the whole fleet was in, except he hadn't seen any carriers lately. It was a lovely night . . . air turning cool as time moved toward midnight.

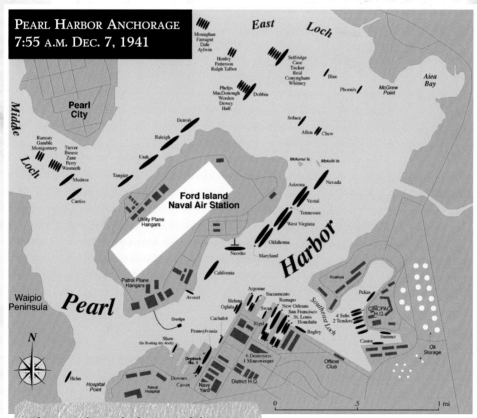

PEARL HARBOR ANCHORAGE
7:55 A.M. DEC. 7, 1941

This map shows the location of the U.S. Navy ships docked at Pearl Harbor right before the first Japanese bombs hit.

Attack! December 7, 1941

On December 7, 1941, an important Japanese message is intercepted in Washington, D.C. It seems to contain information about an attack that will take place at a specific time, but no exact day is indicated. General Marshall the Chief of Staff of the Army, is advised of the message. He tells assistants to communicate with all of the important U.S. bases in the Pacific, including Pearl Harbor. But a series of problems delay the message.

At 6:30 A.M., submarines are detected near the harbor entrance. Japanese **midget submarines** try to sneak into Pearl Harbor and attack. Their attempts are unsuccessful.

At 7:00 A.M., **radar** detects a large number of planes approaching Oahu. A **fleet** of U.S. planes is expected to arrive at Pearl Harbor, so the radar operator does not report the sighting.

At 7:50 A.M., many U.S. sailors are getting ready for church. Some men are still asleep. On the USS *Nevada*, sailors assemble for raising of the flag ceremonies and the playing of the national anthem. In the middle of the anthem, Japanese planes begin bombing and firing.

At 7:55 A.M., the first bombs of the Japanese raid hit. The Ford Island Naval Air Station is hit several times by low-flying planes. Commander Logan Ramsey radios, "AIR RAID ON PEARL HARBOR X THIS IS NOT DRILL". For the next two hours, attacking airplanes roar overhead.

At Wheeler Field, the largest of the airfields protecting Pearl Harbor, men run in all directions as bombs whistle, explosions shake the ground, and fiery flashes of light fill the scene. Men use an ax to break into locked ammunition sheds. But by that time it is too late— most of the attack is over and the airfield is in ruins.

Airfields at Ford Island and other locations have also been attacked. Almost no planes have been able to take off and fight back. The ships in Pearl Harbor are almost defenseless.

A Japanese bomber pilot's account

Haruo Yoshino was a Japanese **torpedo** bomber pilot. As Japanese planes took off, other sailors on the Japanese carriers cheered "Bonzai!" In Japanese, this means "hurrah."

We listened to the radio. The American stations were broadcasting normally [as the attack force flew toward their targets]. So it seemed they were not aware of anything. And that is when I knew that it was going to be a sneak attack.

A soldier's view of the attack

Private Earl M. Schaeffer Jr., a member of the U.S. Army Air Corps, remembers the Japanese attacks he watched firsthand.

Towards 0800 [8:00 A.M.] I heard explosions and aircraft . . . The noises became louder and when things started shaking and rattling and parts of the ceiling coming down, I ran out in the **hangar,** over to the end where the large doors were to see what was the matter. Well, I saw many fires, aircraft burning, buildings afire, much smoke coming from the Pearl Harbor area. It was too much! I just could'nt [couldn't] comprehend just what was going on. I did'nt [didn't] have to wait long to learn the awful truth. Three aircraft came flying very low across the field firing their wing guns at our B-18s, B-17s, and others [types of planes].

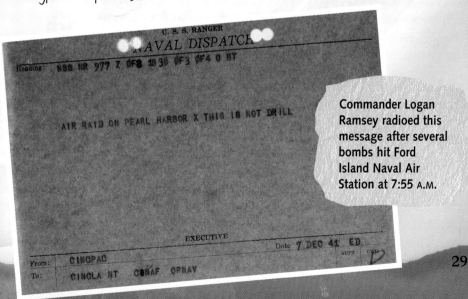

U. S. S. RANGER

NAVAL DISPATCH

Heading: N88 NR 977 Z 0F8 1938 0F3 0F4 0 BT

AIR RAID ON PEARL HARBOR X THIS IS NOT DRILL

EXECUTIVE

Date 7 DEC 41 ED

From: CINCPAC

To: CINCLA NT CONAF OPNAV

Commander Logan Ramsey radioed this message after several bombs hit Ford Island Naval Air Station at 7:55 A.M.

With the Japanese Forces

The Japanese pilots had been aloft by 6:15 A.M. on the morning of December 7. Their air strike force consisted of fighter aircraft, **torpedo** bombers, high-level bombers, and dive-bombers. The pilots had not been permitted to communicate by radio. This was meant to prevent the United States from discovering the 189 pilots in the first wave of attack.

About 90 minutes after the pilots took off, they glimpsed the northern tip of Oahu. The planes split into two groups. One group planned to attack first and hit Wheeler Field. The other group was to head toward the ships in the harbor and attack nearby airfields. By destroying American planes, the Japanese could prevent a defensive attack.

The Japanese pilots saw the ships were **moored** close to each other around Ford Island. This made for easy targets. Target after target was hit and burst into flames, but the U.S. soldiers, sailors, and marines started to recover from their initial surprise. They returned fire from **anti-aircraft guns,** but the Japanese attack had, so far, been a success.

Explosions rock U.S. ships on the far side of Ford Island. A Japanese pilot took this photo.

Commander Fuchida's account

Japanese Air-Attack Commander Mitsuo Fuchida was the leader of the first attack wave of Japanese planes. He was looking through a small peephole in the bottom of his plane as bombs fell toward Pearl Harbor below.

Four bombs in perfect pattern plummeted [fell] like devils of doom. They became small as poppy seeds, and finally disappeared as tiny white flashes of smoke appeared on and near the ship.

Air Commander Mitsuo Fuchida said, "We listened to the radio. American stations were broadcasting normally. It seemed they were not aware of anything."

A Japanese pilot's view of the attack

Haruo Yoshino looked down on Battleship Row from his plane. He aimed at the USS *Oklahoma,* and dropped down to 30 feet (9 meters) above the surface.

It was just as in practice, but right after I dropped my torpedo and turned to the right, I was hit hard by a tremendous sweep of machine-gun fire. Somehow I was able to get out of it. But the telegrapher-radioman behind me was injured, and his radio was broken. I then circled around the lower side of the harbor and out to the assembly point, where we gathered and then headed back to the carriers.

31

Battleships Under Attack

The United States had 185 ships, including 8 of its largest battleships, in Pearl Harbor. This was approximately half of its entire navy. Luckily, the country's three aircraft carriers were not in the harbor. The carriers had received various assignments that took them away from the harbor.

The first battleship hit was the USS *West Virginia*. It sank quickly after being hit by ten bombs. The USS *Oklahoma* was also hit. An eyewitness said, "Then slowly, sickeningly, the *Oklahoma* began to roll over on her side, until, finally only her bottom could be seen." Four hundred fifteen sailors were killed.

The USS *Nevada* tried to escape. As it approached the exit point for the harbor, it was struck by five Japanese bombs. The *Nevada's* crew did not want the ship to block the harbor entrance, so they purposely ran it aground before it sank. By the time the first wave of the attack was over, 21 U.S. ships had been seriously damaged or sunk.

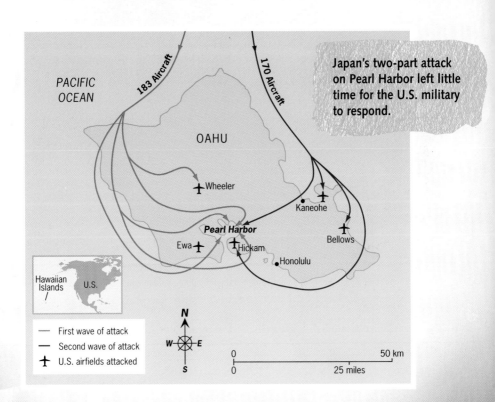

Japan's two-part attack on Pearl Harbor left little time for the U.S. military to respond.

An African-American sailor's account

Torpedo after torpedo struck the USS *West Virginia*. Mess Attendant Second Class Doris (Dorie) Miller and others lifted their wounded captain and carried him to a first-aid post, where he died. Miller, who was a cook onboard, ran to a machine gun. He had not been trained as a gunner because most African-American sailors were only permitted to do noncombat jobs at the start of the war. For his heroism, Miller received the **Navy Cross**. It was the first Navy Cross ever awarded to an African-American sailor.

It wasn't hard. I just pulled the trigger, and she worked fine. I had watched the others with these guns. I guess I fired her for about fifteen minutes. I think I got one of those Jap planes. They were diving pretty close to us.

Doris (Dorie) Miller receives the Navy Cross for heroism.

A sailor describes the attack on the USS *Oklahoma*

Commander Jesse Kenworthy Jr. was serving aboard the USS *Oklahoma* when the Japanese attacked Pearl Harbor. Here, he describes his impressions as the bombs started to fall.

As I reached the upper deck, I felt a very heavy shock and heard a loud explosion and the ship immediately began to list to port [tilt to the left side]. Oil and water descended on the deck and by the time I had reached the boat deck, the shock of two more explosions on the port side was felt. . . . As I attempted to get to the Conning Tower over the decks slippery with oil and water, I felt the shock of another very heavy explosion on the port side.

Onboard the USS *Arizona*

At 7:55 A.M. on December 7, the USS *Arizona* was **moored** in Battleship Row along Ford Island in Pearl Harbor. A repair ship, the *Vestal*, was moored on the other side of the *Arizona*. Suddenly, Japanese **torpedoes** sped underneath the *Vestal* and lodged in the *Arizona*. But the torpedoes were the least of the ship's worries.

At 8:10 A.M., a Japanese plane dropped a 1,764-pound (800-kilogram) bomb on the **forward deck** of the *Arizona*. The impact set off more than one million pounds (454,000 kilograms) of gunpowder that was stored in the ship's **magazine.** Immediately, metal from the ship's deck flew twenty feet (six meters) into the air, and fires began to rage. Even the water surrounding the ship was set ablaze from large oil leaks.

It took just nine minutes for the *Arizona* to sink. Only 337 men survived. Most of the *Arizona's* crew—1,177 men—were killed by the explosion and resulting fire, or were trapped when the ship sank. At the time, the sinking of the *Arizona* was the worst single ship disaster in United States history.

Smoke engulfs the *Arizona* as it tilts and sinks. The *Arizona* was one of many U.S. battleships that sank.

A sailor's view of the attack on the *Arizona*

Carl Carson was a nineteen-year-old sailor onboard the USS *Arizona*. He was able to swim to safety on Ford Island.

I was out on deck doing the morning chores when all of a sudden a plane came along. I didn't pay much attention to it because planes were landing at Ford Island all the time. Then chips started flying all around me. And I realized the plane was strafing [firing at] me. . . . The bomb went off. I guess it knocked me out. I don't know how long I lay there. The water was knee-deep [onboard the ship]. . . . I started to swim to Ford Island. . . . there was oil all around me. And fire all around. A man saw me down there [swimming in the water] and he reached down and pulled me up to the surface.

Senator John McCain's view

John McCain, former member of the U.S. military, is a senator from Arizona. He spoke of the legacy of the USS *Arizona*.

Off Ford Island in Hawaii is the memorial to the USS Arizona, a ship named for the state I am honored to represent in Congress. Parts of its structure emerge from the waters of the **bay** like a cast-iron headstone. The Arizona remains the final resting place for 1,177 of its crew. Sixty years after Japanese bombs sent it to its watery grave, it continues to stand as a silent testament to the sacrifice of so many in defense of liberty. It also serves to remind us of the need to remain **vigilant.**

The USS *Arizona* memorial spans the sunken ship. A smoke stack juts above the water's surface.

35

Two Hours of Destruction

Line after line of Japanese planes pounded targets in and near Pearl Harbor. After months of preparation, the Japanese pilots knew exactly where to go to destroy U.S. ships and planes. They had also practiced how to avoid a collision with other Japanese planes and flew in patterns at different **altitudes**.

Most U.S. ships in the harbor were lined up on Battleship Row in pairs right beside each other. They were so close that explosions and fires spread from one boat to the next. For example, the USS *Arizona* exploded so violently that a huge section of the ship raised several feet in the air before crashing down and sinking. Fiery pieces of the ship flew onto the ship **docked** next to it.

The Japanese attack was quick and very destructive. There was almost no opportunity for the U.S. to counterattack. By the time most survivors were properly organized to fight, the Japanese were gone. When it was over, the airfields and the harbor had several huge fires burning. From start to finish the entire attack had lasted less than two hours.

Below is an airfield on the Ford Island Naval Station after the attack. The U.S. counterattack was slow because guns and ammunition were locked in sheds. The USS *Shaw* explodes in the background.

A sailor's view of the attack on Battleship Row

Charles Christensen was a sailor on the USS *Argonne*, which was **moored** across from Ford Island.

I was . . . putting on my white uniform . . . An explosion slightly shook the ship . . . I wondered what had happened. And I opened the porthole [window] and stuck my head out. And, oh boy, was there ever a fire on Ford Island! I thought, "Wow! I'd better go take a look."

I know it was a Japanese plane, and the **torpedo** was underneath it. It's maybe 30 feet [9 meters] off the water, which puts the pilot maybe eye level with me. I can see the man's face. . . . And he's looking over the side. And when he straightened the plane out, he dropped that torpedo. And that torpedo went as straight for the *Oklahoma* as it could go.

[During the second wave of Japanese attacks] they came down and machine-gunned us. . . . Everything was going off. Our guns were going off. And there were all the explosions over there on Battleship Row. I just couldn't believe all of this was happening in this short length of time. With all of these planes coming in, it looked like bees coming back to the hive. There were so many of them in there at one time it was amazing that they didn't collide.

A survivor's account

George Smith was on the USS *Oklahoma* during the attack.

Then, over the loudspeakers I heard, "All hands man your battle stations." I thought it was another drill.

[Three torpedoes then slammed into the *Oklahoma*.] I was really scared. Then I heard, "Abandon ship." The ship was already rolling over on us. We jumped into the water. It was only about a five-foot [1.5-meter] jump. I saw the ship and the big gun turrets coming down on me, and I began to swim as fast as I could. The ship rolled over. There it was, keel [bottom] up. I was sure that many of my shipmates were trapped inside.

Medical Personnel

The doctors and nurses at Pearl Harbor were also heroes. Thousands of Americans were killed or wounded that day, and the medical personnel stationed at Pearl Harbor worked furiously to save lives.

Because the attack came on a Sunday morning, many doctors and nurses were at home. They raced to the scene in order to treat the victims. Although the Japanese planes did not target hospitals in and near Pearl Harbor, some doctors and nurses came under heavy fire as they moved their patients to safer locations.

Streams of patients began arriving within ten minutes of the first wave of the attack, and the naval hospital did not have room for all of them. Airplane **hangars,** warehouses, ships, and other forms of shelter were turned into makeshift hospitals because of the massive amount of wounded. The most common cases were **shrapnel** wounds and extensive burns. By midnight on December 7, more than 950 patients were in the naval hospital alone.

The nurses and doctors at Pearl Harbor faced tremendous hardships that day. They were forced to deal with a shortage of equipment, an overwhelming number of patients, and fatal injuries. Yet they worked to the best of their abilities and saved hundreds of lives.

Sandbags protect this naval field hospital in Oahu. An air raid shelter was built underneath to protect people and important supplies, like blood.

An army nurse's account

Second Lieutenant Madelyn Blonskey was assigned to the Army Nurse Corps at Tripler Army Hospital, located about six miles (9.7 kilometers) from Battleship Row.

About 8:20 A.M. the on-call nurse in the operating room at Tripler called me, very upset and anxious. She said a soldier had told her Pearl Harbor was being attacked.

I hurried toward the side entrance of the hospital and started up the stairs to a second-floor porch. As I reached the top of the stairs—I will never forget what I saw—there were about 15 or 20 stretchers with injured men lying on them. They were lined up head to toe next to the railing of the porch. There were more bloody wounds—caused by shrapnel—than I had ever seen in my life.

We started operating. The air-raid sirens blew. And we heard the roar of planes over the fragile wooden hospital. We had nowhere to go. We had a patient in the middle of an operation. The big [Japanese] bombers, heading for Pearl Harbor, flew so low that the vibrations shook the instruments on the table.

I was scared. I said to the surgeon, "Colonel, I know God knows we did nothing to deserve this. And I am putting my trust in Him." Then the last plane flew over and everything was silent.

Caring for the wounded and dying went on for days. Schools were made into temporary emergency rooms. The cafeteria was used for the operating room, and the kitchen was used for sterilizing instruments [making them germ-free]. There were shortages of bandages and medicines. We were not prepared for the many hundreds of casualties.

Aftermath

By the time the attack ended, 2,403 Americans (including civilians) had been killed and 1,178 were wounded. Much of the United States's Navy **fleet** was destroyed. Twenty-one vessels had either been sunk or were badly damaged. The airfields also sustained heavy damage, and nearly 350 planes had been destroyed or damaged. The *Japan Times and Advertiser* ran the headline "U.S. Pacific Fleet is Wiped Out!" The newspaper went on to describe the attack and claimed that Japan had "reduced the U.S. to a third-class power overnight." **Prime Minister** Tojo went on the radio to formally declare war against the United States.

One U.S. soldier wrote about the aftermath: "[It was] a ghastly sight of sunken ships . . . oil covered water . . ."

General Yamamoto, who planned the Pearl Harbor attack, said, "I fear we have only awakened a sleeping giant and filled him with terrible resolve [determination]." He was right. Yamamoto found out that the U.S. aircraft carriers had not been found and destroyed. This major **objective** of the attack was not completed. Also, the ship-repair facilities at Pearl Harbor had not been seriously damaged. Many ships that had been bombed were fixed and back in operation sooner than the Japanese expected.

On December 7, 1941, the same day as the assault on Pearl Harbor, Japan also launched attacks on the Philippines and other Southeast Asian sites. Great Britain, Australia, and other nations joined the United States against Japan in the War for the Pacific. In the year following Pearl Harbor, the **Allies** experienced defeat after defeat against overwhelming numbers of Japanese soldiers.

Japanese messages from Pearl Harbor

In Japan, Admiral Yamamoto listened to Lieutenant Commander Yasuji Watanabe as he relayed radio messages from Pearl Harbor.

"Battleship *Pennsylvania*, direct hit!"

"Battleship *West Virginia*, sunk!"

"Cruiser *Helena*, heavy damage!"

"Battleship *Oklahoma*, capsized!"

A sailor's account from the USS *Oklahoma*

Seaman Joseph Hdruska, 22, boarded the USS *Oklahoma* after the attacks in a rescue operation.

I was terribly afraid. We were cutting through with acetylene [welding] torches. First we found six naked men waist deep in water. They didn't know how long they had been down there and they were crying and moaning with pain. Some of them were very badly wounded. We could hear tapping all over the ship, SOS taps, no voices, just those eerie taps from all over. There was nothing we could do for most of them.

A radioman's account

Radioman First Class Raymond M. Tufteland of the United States Navy described the scene five days after the attack.

Our force entered Pearl [Harbor] to witness a ghastly sight of sunken ships—oil-covered water—wreckage and ruins. We first passed the *Nevada* which had been beached to prevent sinking. Next one was *California*—badly damaged and on bottom. The hull of the *Oklahoma* then came in sight after having capsized. The *Tennessee* and *West Virginia* behind here were both damaged. . . . The *Arizona* was completely blown up and a twisted mass of iron . . . Bodies were still being taken from ships and out of the water a week after attack. It was a sight none of us like to remember.

The United States Reacts

People on the United States mainland—more than 2,000 miles (3,219 kilometers) away from Pearl Harbor—started to hear about the attacks within 90 minutes. They were shocked. President Franklin D. Roosevelt acted quickly.

Very few people owned television sets in 1941, so President Roosevelt made a radio address. The president condemned the actions of the Japanese military. He then asked U.S. citizens to join in the effort to defeat their country's new enemy, Japan. Most people knew that this would also mean a war with Germany, Japan's ally.

The **economic** problems caused by the **Great Depression** and the number of U.S. soldiers killed during World War I (1914–1918) had prompted the United States to adopt a **policy** known as **isolationism** throughout the 1920s and 1930s. This meant that the country focused primarily on itself and not on the issues of other nations. Although many Americans were surprised at the type of attack that was carried out at Pearl Harbor, they were not surprised to hear that the United States was officially entering the conflict. Much of the world was already at war.

Within a few weeks, U.S. factories were changed so they could produce war supplies. Young men volunteered to fight or were **drafted** into military service. Women filled jobs while servicemen were away. Other women joined the service as nurses and in positions behind the lines of battle. Even children helped by growing extra vegetables in their gardens, by collecting scrap metal for recycling, and by writing letters to cheer up soldiers who were far from home.

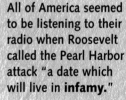

All of America seemed to be listening to their radio when Roosevelt called the Pearl Harbor attack "a date which will live in **infamy**."

An address by President Franklin Roosevelt

At 12:09 P.M. on December 8, 1941, the day after Pearl Harbor, President Roosevelt entered the chamber of the House of Representatives in the Capitol. Shortly after, he addressed the members of Congress.

Yesterday, December 7, 1941—a date which will live in infamy— the United States of America was suddenly and deliberately attacked by the naval and air forces of the Empire of Japan. … The attack yesterday … has caused severe damage to American naval and military forces. Very many American lives have been lost. … With confidence in our armed forces—with the unbounded determination of our people— we will gain the inevitable triumph—so help us God.

A senator asks questions

Senator Thomas Connally was the chairman of the Senate Foreign Relations Committee from 1941 to 1947. In a meeting after the attack on Pearl Harbor, he spoke harshly to Frank Knox, Secretary of the Navy:

Why did you have all the ships at Pearl Harbor crowded in the way you did? … I am amazed by the attack by Japan, but I am still more astounded at what happened to our Navy. They were all asleep. Where were our patrols?

With so many men fighting in the war, women were trained to work in factories.

Fighting Back and the Japanese Surrender

By the evening of December 7, 1941, almost everyone in the United States knew what had happened at Pearl Harbor. The sense of loss was overwhelming. How could so many loved ones, neighbors, and young servicemen abruptly be gone? Americans became determined to win World War II (1939–1945). "Remember Pearl Harbor!" became a rallying cry as U.S. soldiers, sailors, and marines joined the **Allied** forces to fight back against Japan and the **Axis** powers.

The shipyards at Pearl Harbor rebuilt and repaired ships as quickly as possible. Within six months, the U.S. Navy was almost as strong as it was before the attack. Although the U.S. Navy was rebuilt, the Philippines, Singapore, and several other Southeast Asian lands fell to the Japanese during 1941 and 1942. From June 3 through June 6, 1942, however, the U.S. defeated Japan during the Battle of Midway. That defeat—during which Japan lost much of its naval power—stopped their advance in Southeast Asia. The Allies then began the drive toward a final victory over the Axis powers.

Posters like this urged support for the war effort. The tragedy of Pearl Harbor was not to be forgotten.

...we here highly resolve that these dead shall not have died in vain...

REMEMBER DEC. 7th!

On September 2, 1945, the leaders of Japan formally surrendered. Japanese Foreign Minister Mamoru Shigemitsu led nine representatives from Japan to sign a **treaty** aboard the USS *Missouri* in Tokyo Bay. Leaders from Japan, the United States, China, Great Britain, Australia, and the Soviet Union were present.

General MacArthur's address

General Douglas MacArthur had been in charge of all Allied forces in the Southwest Pacific Theater. He represented the Allies at Japan's surrender.

We are gathered here ... to conclude a solemn agreement whereby peace may be restored ... It is my earnest hope and indeed the hope of all mankind that from this ... occasion a better world shall emerge out of the blood and carnage [killings] of the past—a world founded upon faith and understanding—a world dedicated to the dignity of man around the fulfillment of his most cherished wish—for freedom, tolerance, and justice.

Aboard the USS *Missouri* Japanese officials sign surrender documents ending World War II as Allied officers and crew decks watch in silence.

Japanese Americans After Pearl Harbor

After the attacks on Pearl Harbor, many U.S. government officials and regular citizens believed that Japanese Americans could not be trusted. They thought that Japanese Americans would try to help Japan win its fight against the United States. This feeling was especially strong in California, Arizona, Oregon, and Washington, all of which had substantial Japanese-American populations. Hawaii—a U.S. territory at the time of the attack—was also home to many people of Japanese descent.

The anti-Japanese hysteria led President Franklin D. Roosevelt to sign Executive Order 9066 on February 19, 1942. This order forced more than 100,000 people of Japanese ancestry, most of whom were American citizens, to leave their homes on the West Coast and move to **internment camps.** These people were given only a few days to register with the government before being moved from their homes by armed guards. Interestingly, Americans of German or Italian descent were permitted to stay, even though the United States was also at war with Germany and Italy.

Civil Liberties Act of 1988

It was not until the war ended in 1945 that these Japanese Americans were permitted to leave the camps. In 1988, almost 50 years after the war ended, Congress passed the Civil Liberties Act of 1988. The act required Congress to pay $20,000 to each person who had been interned during the war. The act recognized that "a grave injustice" had been done to the Japanese-American population. Ronald Reagan, the president of the United States at that time, also sent a signed apology on behalf of the American people.

SOLD
by White & Pollard

GROCERY WA

FRUITS
AND
VEGETABLES

I AM AN AMERICAN

WANTO CO. WANTO CO.

Interned Japanese-Americans had to pack their belongings, close their businesses, and sell or rent their homes and equipment in a short amount of time.

A Japanese American's view

In 1941, seventeen-year-old Daniel Inouye—a Japanese-American—lived in Honolulu, Hawaii. He volunteered to fight in World War II along with more than 2,500 other Japanese Americans. He was awarded the Congressional Medal of Honor for his actions during the World War II raid in which he lost his arm. After the war, Daniel decided to go into politics. He was elected to the House of Representatives and then to the Senate. There, he has dedicated his life to avoid future wars, promote harmony between races, and assist in peace talks between nations.

It was a bright Sunday morning. . . . I rushed outside, stood in the warm sunshine by the side of our house, and watched in horror as the planes . . . dive-bombed and fired on the U.S. Pacific **Fleet moored** at Pearl Harbor. . . . The secretary of the Red Cross telephoned to enlist my help, since I had recently begun teaching first aid. I immediately got on my bicycle and rushed to the aid station at my childhood school. Fortunately for me and my family, the military leaders in Hawaii did not intern us [send them to an internment camp].

A student's view

Dellie Hahne, a 21-year-old music major at Santa Barbara State College at the time of the Pearl Harbor attack, commented on anti-Japanese feelings.

In an incredibly short time . . . a wave of patriotism swept the country. As we drove home we felt, "This is our country, and we're going to fight to defend it" . . . The next day we all returned to classes, but there was a Japanese student in my art class who stayed in her room and was afraid to leave because of the attack. The art teacher mentioned this to us and we all thought, "Well, she should." We had no understanding, no pity, no tolerance.

What Happened to the Leaders?

After President Franklin D. Roosevelt made his now-famous speech on December 8, 1941, Congress voted to declare war on Japan. President Roosevelt was reelected to the presidency for a fourth term in 1944 and helped to lead the United States to victory in 1945.

Admiral Isoroku Yamamoto had been the mastermind behind the attack on Pearl Harbor. After the attack, Yamamoto felt that the only way for Japan to win the war would be for it to destroy the remains of the U.S. **fleet.** Japan again took on the United States during the Battle of Midway in 1942, which was won by the U.S. Yamamoto was killed when U.S. forces shot down his plane over the Solomon Islands on April 18, 1943.

Admiral Chuichi Nagumo had carried out the successful December 7 attack on Pearl Harbor. On June 4, 1942, Nagumo's forces were defeated by the United States during the Battle of Midway. On July 6, 1944, Nagumo committed suicide during the end stages of the Japanese defense of Saipan.

Prime Minister and Minister of War Hideki Tojo continued to lead Japan's war efforts after Pearl Harbor. He was responsible for important Japanese victories in Southeast Asia and the Pacific. By 1944, a series of Japanese losses resulted in decreased military and public support for Tojo. On September 11, 1945, Tojo attempted to commit suicide. He was nursed back to health and put on trial for **war crimes** before the International Military **Tribunal** for the Far East. The Tribunal found him guilty, and he was hanged.

Admiral Kimmel and General Short, the commanders at Pearl Harbor, were assigned most of the blame for the disastrous results of the attacks. They were removed from command and stripped of their ranks. Kimmel and Short did make serious mistakes; however, there were others who also had performed poorly. On October 30, 2000, almost 60 years after the attacks, President Bill Clinton signed into law the National Defense Authorization Act. Part of the Act states that Kimmel and Short were not given the information necessary for them to have prevented the attacks on Pearl Harbor.

An address by Emperor Hirohito

On August 15, 1945, Emperor Hirohito made a radio address during which he accepted the Potsdam Declaration.

We have ordered our Government to communicate to the Governments of the United States, Great Britain, China, and the Soviet Union that our empire accepts the provisions of their joint declaration. . . .

Indeed, we declared war on America and Britain out of our sincere desire to insure Japan's self-preservation and the stabilization of East Asia, it being far from our thought either to infringe upon the sovereignty [power] of other nations or to embark upon territorial aggrandizement [enlarging the country].

But now the war has lasted for nearly four years. Despite the best that has been done by everyone . . . the war situation has developed not necessarily to Japan's advantage, while the general trends of the world have all turned against her interest. . . .

General Douglas MacArthur meets with Hirohito at the U.S. embassy in Tokyo. MacArthur was in charge of the U.S. occupation of Japan after WWII.

Let the entire nation continue as one family from generation to generation, ever firm in its faith of the imperishableness [longevity] of its divine land, and mindful of its heavy burden of responsibilities, and the long road before it. Unite your total strength to be devoted to the construction for the future. Cultivate the ways of rectitude [righteousness], nobility of spirit, and work with resolution [determination] so that you may enhance the innate glory of the Imperial State and keep pace with the progress of the world.

What Have We Learned from Pearl Harbor?

The "date which will live in **infamy**" can teach us many lessons. We learned that our country should always be prepared and that we should never underestimate the abilities of an enemy. We also learned that we should make sure military communications are efficient.

History teaches us to learn from past mistakes. The Alamo (1836) and the Vietnam War (1955–1975) were huge disasters. The United States learned from each of these incidents and brought about great victories. Defeat at the Alamo motivated Texans to win independence from Mexico. Lessons learned in Vietnam helped leaders in the Persian Gulf War in 1991 to win.

The young American women and men who survived Pearl Harbor never forgot it. Almost all said the event affected them for the rest of their lives. Many continue to speak of the event to others and of the importance of being prepared. Others simply spread a message that all people should work for peace.

This aerial view of Tokyo, Japan, shows the extensive damage caused by American air raid attacks during WWII.

Daniel Inouye's account

Now a 79 year-old senator from Hawaii, David Inouye still remembers the attack, which happened near his home.

I will never forget that Sunday morning, and I hope that my fellow Americans will remember Pearl Harbor and its many lessons forever. To forget Pearl Harbor is to forget the good and evil that human beings are capable of in times of crisis. Without a vivid memory of this event, we may lack the fortitude [strong will] and the preparedness to withstand future assaults [attacks] on our country and its democratic ideals.

Perhaps the best lessons of Pearl Harbor come from those who witnessed the attack and took part in WWII. Listening to the words of those who experienced Pearl Harbor can help us be better prepared in the future.

Timeline

1853	Commodore Matthew Perry arrives in Tokyo and demands that Japan begin trading with the United States
1868	Emperor Mutsuhito reestablishes the Japanese monarchy; promotes western ideas, institutions, and technologies
1878	The Japanese army is no longer controlled by lawmakers—they are independent
1898	The United States makes Hawaii a territory
1910	Japan takes over Korea
1914–1918	Japan seizes German possessions in China and East Asia
1931	Japan conquers Manchuria, China
1932	Military leaders become dominant in Japanese government and disputes lead to Japan leaving the **League of Nations**
1932	Hitler takes power in Germany
1936	The Japanese navy is greatly expanded and modernized
1937	Japan attacks and expands into more of China; Roosevelt condemns the action
1938	World War II begins in Europe with Hitler's invasion of Poland
1940	Pearl Harbor becomes the main U.S. base for its Pacific **Fleet;** the United States stops trading metal goods and oil to Japan, and Japan becomes allied with Germany and Italy
1941	January 27: Joseph Grew, U.S. **ambassador** to Japan, says the Japanese have a plan to attack Pearl Harbor
	July 24: Japan gains complete control of **Indochina**
	July 26: President Roosevelt halts U.S. trade with Japan
	October 18: General Hideki Tojo becomes **prime minister** of Japan
	November 7: The Japanese secretly set December 7 as the date for an attack on Pearl Harbor
	November 20: Ambassador Kichisaburo Nomura and special envoy Saburo Kurusu begin talks with U.S. Secretary of State Cordell Hull
	November 25: Japanese fleet leaves for Pearl Harbor
	December 6: Roosevelt appeals to Emperor Hirohito to prevent war
	December 7: The Japanese launch attacks on Pearl Harbor, the Philippines, Wake, Guam, Midway Islands, Hong Kong, Malaya, and Thailand
	December 8: The United States declares war on Japan
1942	February 19: President Roosevelt signs Executive Order 9066, forcing people of Japanese ancestry living in the U.S. to move into **internment camps**
	June 3–6: The U.S. defeats Japan during the Battle of Midway
1943	April 18: Admiral Isoroku Yamamoto is killed when U.S. forces shoot down his plane over the Solomon Islands
1944	President Roosevelt is reelected as president for a fourth term
1945	April 12: Franklin Roosevelt dies. Vice President Truman becomes President of the United States
	May 7: Germany surrenders and World War II in Europe ends
	August 14: Japan formally surrenders to the United States
	September 2: Japanese officials sign the statement of surrender. President Truman declares V-J Day (Victory over Japan Day) and World War II ends
1948	December 23: Hideki Tojo is hanged after being convicted as a war criminal by the International Military **Tribunal** for the Far East

List of Primary Sources

The author and publisher gratefully acknowledge the following publications and websites from which written sources in this book are drawn. In some cases, the wording or sentence structure has been simplified to make the material more appropriate for a school readership.

p. 9 Fortune Magazine, 1940: *Pearl Harbor: America's Darkest Day,* Susan Wells (New York: Time-Life Books, 2001).
   John Rampley: *Pearl Harbor: America's Darkest Day,* Susan Wells (New York: Time-Life Books, 2001).
p. 11 Edwin Reischauer: *My Life Between Japan and America,* Edwin O. Reischauer (New York: Harper and Row, 1987)
p. 13 Adolf Hitler: *Man's Unfinished Journey: A World History,* Marvin Perry (Boston: Houghton Mifflin Company, 1978).
p. 15 Sho Tokutomi: *At Dawn We Slept: The Untold Story of Pearl Harbor,* Gordon W. Prange (New York: McGraw Hill Book Co., 1981).
   Ambassador Joseph Grew: *Pearl Harbor: The Day of Infamy, An Illustrated History,* Dan Van Der Vat (Toronto: Basic Books/Madison Press Book, 2001).
   Captain Hideo Hiraide: *Milestones of History: Decades of Crises,* Roger Morgan, Ed. (New York: Newsweek Books, 1975).
p. 17 Minoru Genda: *Pearl Harbor: The Day of Infamy, An Illustrated History,* Dan Van Der Vat (Toronto: Basic Books/Madison Press Book, 2001).
p. 19 Admiral Husband Kimmel: *Long Day's Journey Into War: December 7, 1941,* Stanley Weintraub (New York: Truman Talley Books, 1991).
   General Dwight Eisenhower: *Dec. 7, 1941: The Day the Japanese Attacked Pearl Harbor,* Gordon W. Prange (New York: McGraw Hill, 1988).
p. 21 Admiral Isoroku Yamamoto: *Milestones of History: Decades of Crises,* Roger Morgan, Ed. (New York: Newsweek Books, 1975).
   Emperor Hirohito: to members at a cabinet meeting (September 1941).
p. 23 Cordell Hull: to British ambassador to the United States, Lord Halifax (January 1941).
p. 25 Japanese Foreign Ministry: *At Dawn We Slept: The Untold Story of Pearl Harbor,* Gordon W. Prange (New York: McGraw Hill Book Co., 1981).
p. 27 Ed Sheehan: *Long Day's Journey Into War: December 7, 1941,* Stanley Weintraub (New York: Truman Talley Books, 1991).
p. 29 Haruo Yoshino: *Remember Pearl Harbor: Americans and Japanese Survivors Tell Their Stories,* Thomas B. Allen (Washington, D.C.: National Geographic Society, 2001).
   Earl M. Schaeffer, Jr.: "World War II: Personal Accounts, Pearl Harbor to V-J Day," traveling exhibition, The Lyndon Baines Johnson Foundation: National Archives and Records Administration.
p. 31 Mitsuo Fuchida: *Remember Pearl Harbor: Americans and Japanese Survivors Tell Their Stories,* Thomas B. Allen (Washington, D.C.: National Geographic Society, 2001).
   Haruo Yoshino: *Remember Pearl Harbor: Americans and Japanese Survivors Tell Their Stories,* Thomas B. Allen (Washington, D.C.: National Geographic Society, 2001).
p. 33 Dorie Miller: *Remember Pearl Harbor: Americans and Japanese Survivors Tell Their Stories,* Thomas B. Allen (Washington, D.C.: National Geographic Society, 2001).
   Jesse Kenworthy, Jr.: *World War II: The War in the Pacific,* Don Nardo (Farmington Hills, Mich.: Lucent Books, 1991).
p. 35 Carl Carson: *Remember Pearl Harbor: Americans and Japanese Survivors Tell Their Stories,* Thomas B. Allen (Washington, D.C.: National Geographic Society, 2001).
   Senator John McCain: *Pearl Harbor: The Day of Infamy, An Illustrated History,* Dan Van Der Vat (Toronto: Basic Books/Madison Press Book, 2001).
p. 37 Charles Christensen: *Remember Pearl Harbor: Americans and Japanese Survivors Tell Their Stories,* Thomas B. Allen (Washington, D.C.: National Geographic Society, 2001).
   George Smith: *Remember Pearl Harbor: Americans and Japanese Survivors Tell Their Stories,* Thomas B. Allen (Washington, D.C.: National Geographic Society, 2001).
p. 39 Madelyn Blonsky: *Remember Pearl Harbor: Americans and Japanese Survivors Tell Their Stories,* Thomas B. Allen (Washington, D.C.: National Geographic Society, 2001).
p. 41 Joseph Hdruska: *Remember Pearl Harbor: Americans and Japanese Survivors Tell Their Stories,* Thomas B. Allen (Washington, D.C.: National Geographic Society, 2001).
   Raymond M. Tufteland: *Remember Pearl Harbor: Americans and Japanese Survivors Tell Their Stories,* Thomas B. Allen (Washington, D.C.: National Geographic Society, 2001).
p. 43 Franklin Roosevelt: *Dec. 7, 1941: The Day the Japanese Attacked Pearl Harbor,* Gordon W. Prange (New York: McGraw Hill, 1988).
   Senator Thomas Connally: *December 7, 1941, Pearl Harbor: America's Darkest Day,* Susan Wells (New York: Time-Life Books, 2001).
p. 45 General Douglas MacArthur: *World War II: The War in the Pacific,* Don Nardo (Farmington Hills, Mich.: Lucent Books, 1991).
p. 47 Senator Daniel Inouye: *December 7, 1941, Pearl Harbor: America's Darkest Day*, Susan Wells (New York: Time-Life Books, 2001).
   Dellie Hahne: *The Home Front: America During World War II,* Mark J. Harris, Franklin D. Mitchell, and Steven J. Schechter (New York: Putnam's and Sons, 1984).
p. 49 Emperor Hirohito: from radio broadcast accepting Potsdam Declaration (August 14, 1945).
p. 51 Senator Daniel Inouye: *December 7, 1941, Pearl Harbor: America's Darkest Day,* Susan Wells (New York: Time-Life Books, 2001).

Glossary

adjacent immediately next to aircraft carrier ship used as a mobile base for airplanes

Allies during World War II, the countries that fought against the Axis powers, including Great Britain, France, the United States, and the Soviet Union

altitude height above sea level

anti-aircraft gun quick-firing, small cannon designed to shoot down airplanes

ambassador person sent as the chief representative of his or her government in another country

Axis describing the military forces of Germany, Italy, Japan, and the countries that fought with them during World War II

barbarian uncivilized person

bay narrow arm of water that juts inland

bias existing opinion about someone or something that makes it hard to be fair

Cabinet U.S. government officials appointed to be the President's closest advisors and leaders of certain government departments

commander in chief person who holds supreme command of the armed forces of a nation

comply act in agreement with a command

conquer defeat

deteriorate get worse

dictator person who has absolute control of a government

Diet group of lawmakers in Japan's national government similar to Congress or Parliament

diplomat government official who handles the relations of his or her country with other countries

dock to position for loading or unloading

draft to call up for required military service

dry-dock dock that is kept dry and used for repairing and building ships

economy system for organizing businesses, finances, and resources in a country

expansionist person who believed more territory should be acquired

export to send goods to another country for sale; or, one of those goods sent

fascism form of government usually headed by a dictator, in which the government controls most aspects of the people's lives

fleet group of warships under one command; a country's navy

forward deck front deck on a ship

Great Depression worldwide economic downturn of the 1930s

hangar enclosed area for holding and repairing aircraft

hysteria extreme commotion

import to bring in goods from another country for sale; or, one of those goods brought in

Indochina land that once included the countries of Vietnam, Laos, and Cambodia

infamy extreme disgrace

internment camp temporary holding area for groups thought to be a threat

isolation being set apart

isolationism policy of staying completely out of the affairs of other nations

League of Nations organization of international cooperation established at the end of World War I (1914–1918)

magazine structure that stores arms and ammunition

midget submarines small underwater vessels operated by only two persons

military dictator leader in the armed forces who also has complete power and control of a nation

moored tied up securely

natural resource material found in nature that is useful or necessary for life

Navy Cross award given by the navy to people who distinguish themselves in action by heroism

Nazi member of the National Socialist German Workers' Party; supporter of Adolf Hitler

negotiate have a discussion with another in order to settle something

objective purpose; goal

pact agreement

policy course of action chosen to guide people in making decisions

prejudice belief that one group is superior to another

profit valuable gain, usually in money

prime minister leader of a nation's lawmaking body who acts similar to a president

radar detection system using radio waves. Radio waves are projected and will "bounce" back to a machine when they hit objects. The machine displays the objects on a screen.

raw material basic material needed to produce goods

resign give up by a formal or official act; quit

restrictive limiting

Roman Empire lands and people under the rule of ancient Rome

sabotage secretly using violent and destructive acts; one who performs sabotage is a saboteur

shrapnel pieces that scatter when an explosive shell hits the ground or an object

standard of living the way of living that a community considers necessary to provide enough things for the people's well being

torpedo bomb that moves through water because of a propeller on its rear portion

treaty treaty between two or more states or countries

tribunal court of justice

tropical climate long-term weather that is rainy and hot

vigilant very alert

war crime crime—such as maltreatment of prisoners—committed during or in connection with war

Sources for Further Research

Barr, Gary E. *World War II Home Front.* Chicago: Heinemann Library, 2004.

Chorlton, Windsor. *Weapons and Technology of World War II.* Chicago: Heinemann Library, 2002.

Reynoldson, Fiona. *Key Battles of World War II.* Chicago: Heinemann Library, 2001.

Tames, Richard. *Pearl Harbor: The U.S. Enters World War II.* Chicago: Heinemann Library, 2001.

Index